¡Ven conmigo!®

Adelante

Holt Spanish Level 1A

Grammar & Vocabulary
Workbook

HOLT, RINEHART AND WINSTON
Harcourt Brace & Company

Austin · New York · Orlando · Atlanta · San Francisco · Boston · Dallas · Toronto · London

PHOTO/ART CREDITS
Abbreviations used: (c) center, (l) left, (r) right, (bkgd) background

Photo Credits
All pre-Columbian symbols by EclectiCollections/HRW.
Front cover: (bkgd), © Robert Fried; (c), Joe Viesti/Viesti Associates, Inc.

Art Credits
All work, unless otherwise noted, contributed by Holt, Rinehart & Winston.

Printed in the United States of America

ISBN 0-03-052279-X

1 2 3 4 5 6 021 02 01 00 99 98

Contents

CAPÍTULO 1 ¡Mucho gusto!

■ PRIMER PASO

To say hello and goodbye, to introduce people, and to ask how someone is, you'll need to use greetings and other courtesy expressions. You'll also need to use the subject pronouns **tú** and **yo**.

 **ASÍ SE DICE** Greetings *Pupil's Edition, p. 27*

1 Chen is spending a semester at a high school in Mexico. How would Chen respond to each of the following expressions? Write an appropriate answer for each one.

1. Buenos días, Chen. _____

2. Hasta luego. _____

3. Adiós. _____

4. Tengo que irme. _____

5. Bueno, tengo clase. _____

 **ASÍ SE DICE** Introducing people *Pupil's Edition, p. 29*

2 During Chen's semester at the Mexican high school, he meets many new students. Use the words in the word box to complete his dialogue with Raimundo, a fellow student.

amiga	soy	amigo	se	amigos
gusto	llamas	llamo	igualmente	

RAIMUNDO ¿Y tú? ¿Cómo te **(1)** _____?

CHEN Me **(2)** _____ Chen.

RAIMUNDO **(3)** _____ Raimundo Gutiérrez. Éstos son mis

(4) _____. Éste es mi **(5)** _____

Pablo. Ésta es mi **(6)** _____ Raquel.

CHEN ¡Mucho **(7)** _____!

RAQUEL **(8)** _____.

Gramática Spanish punctuation *Pupil's Edition, p. 30*

- Notice the upside down punctuation marks in Spanish.

  ¿Cómo te llamas?   **¡Mucho gusto!**

- In Spanish, an accent mark is sometimes used over vowels (**á, é, í, ó, ú**) to show which syllable in a word is stressed. The letter **ñ** has a tilde (**~**) over it to show that it is pronounced like the *ny* in the word *canyon*.

3 Paulette forgot to put in punctuation in her Spanish homework. Change the following sentences to questions (**Q**) or exclamations (**E**) using the correct punctuation.

1. (E) _____ Hola _____

2. (Q) _____ Hay una carta para mí _____

3. (E) _____ Yo soy Francisco _____

4. (Q) _____ Y tú _____

5. (Q) _____ Qué tal _____

4 Paulette also forgot to include accents in her assignment! Help her out by rewriting the following words using accents for the vowel in the stressed syllable. *Hint:* The stressed syllable is indicated by bold-faced letters.

MODELO a**tun** = a**tún**

   como = **có**mo

1. Ve**ro**nica _____

2. Benja**min** _____

3. per**don** _____

4. vio**lin** _____

5. **ma**scara _____

6. **lam**para _____

7. te**le**fono _____

8. heli**cop**tero _____

9. veinti**dos** _____

10. **a**guila _____

5 Read the following dialogue between Maureen, Greg, and Denise and rewrite all of the words with missing accents and punctuation marks. *Hint:* There are 6 accents missing. You'll need to mark your paper 8 times.

MAUREEN Hola. _____

   GREG Buenos dias. _____

MAUREEN Esta es mi amiga Denise. _____

   GREG Mucho gusto!, Denise. _____

 DENISE Encantada. Eh, perdon. Como te llamas tu? _____

   GREG Me llamo Greg. _____

MAUREEN Bueno, tengo clase. Tengo que irme. _____

   GREG Hasta luego, Maureen. _____

MAUREEN Adios. _____

 **ASÍ SE DICE** Greetings *Pupil's Edition, p. 31*

6 Berta loves creating crossword puzzles! Can you solve her latest puzzle?

Horizontales *(Across)*

3. Yo _____ *(too)*.
4. ¿Cómo _____?
6. _____ mal.
7. Excelente = _____.

Verticales *(Down)*

1. ¿_____ tal?
2. Estoy _____ bien, gracias.
4. _____ bien.
5. Más o _____.

7 Write the appropriate question or answer that would correspond to each of the following items. Remember to punctuate correctly.

1. ¿Qué tal?

2. Estoy bastante bien. ¿Y tú?

3. ¿Cómo estás?

4. _____ / Estoy muy mal.

5. _____ / Estoy muy bien.

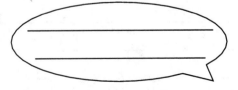
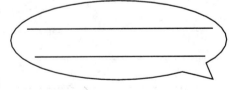

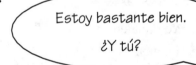

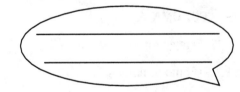
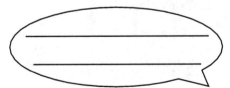

Gramática Subject pronouns **tú** and **yo** *Pupil's Edition, p. 32*

- The pronoun **yo,** capitalized only at the beginning of a sentence, is used when you refer to yourself: **Yo soy Mariela.**
- The pronoun **tú** is used when you are talking to a friend or a classmate. **¿Y tú?**
- The pronouns **tú** and **yo** can either be stated or implied.

  Yo is implied in the following expressions: **Bueno, tengo clase; Tengo que irme; Me llamo... ; Soy... ;** and **Estoy bien, gracias.**

  Tú is implied in these expressions: **¿Cómo te llamas?** and **¿Cómo estás?**

8 María Elena and José Antonio have just met at school. Read their conversation and, in the blanks provided, write the pronoun implied in each exchange.

MARÍA ELENA   ¡Hola! ¿Cómo estás hoy? **(1)** _____

JOSÉ ANTONIO   Hola. Estoy muy bien, gracias. **(2)** _____

MARÍA ELENA   A ver... ¿Cómo te llamas? **(3)** _____

JOSÉ ANTONIO   Me llamo José Antonio González. **(4)** _____

MARÍA ELENA   Soy María Elena Ramírez. Mucho gusto. **(5)** _____

JOSÉ ANTONIO   Igualmente. ¡Uf! Tengo clase ahora. **(6)** _____

MARÍA ELENA   Ah, sí. Tengo que irme también. Hasta mañana, ¿eh? **(7)** _____

9 Vivián is getting to know her classmates. Match each of her questions and statements (Column A) with the responses her classmates give (Column B).

COLUMN A	COLUMN B
_____ 1. Éste es mi amigo, Raúl.	**a.** Yo también.
_____ 2. ¿Cómo te llamas?	**b.** Regular.
_____ 3. Estoy bien.	**c.** Se llama Francisco.
_____ 4. ¿Cómo estás?	**d.** Muy bien.
_____ 5. ¿Qué tal?	**e.** ¡Mucho gusto!
	f. Soy Mónica Sánchez.

10 What expressions would you use...?

1. when greeting a friend _____

2. when introducing yourself _____

3. to respond to someone's introduction _____

4. when you have to leave _____

5. to excuse yourself _____

6. to say that you're doing well _____

■ SEGUNDO PASO

To say how old someone is, you'll need to use the numbers from 0 to 30. To ask where someone is from, you'll need to use the verb **ser** and to be able to form a question.

VOCABULARIO   Numbers from 0 to 30   *Pupil's Edition, p. 36*

11 Simón is working in the school bookstore taking orders for yearbooks over the phone. For each number of yearbooks ordered, write the correct numeral.

1. cinco _____
2. diez _____
3. veintiuno _____
4. ocho _____
5. siete _____

6. treinta _____
7. dieciocho _____
8. quince _____
9. veintiséis _____
10. trece _____

12 Simón's boss wants to know how many yearbooks have been ordered by each customer. Help Simón by writing the following numbers in Spanish words.

1. 8 _____
2. 2 _____
3. 12 _____
4. 20 _____
5. 16 _____

6. 22 _____
7. 26 _____
8. 17 _____
9. 4 _____
10. 30 _____

13 Claudia needs help with her math problems. Help her solve these math problems by filling in the blanks with the correct words.

MODELO   2 + 3 = **dos** y **tres** son **cinco**

1. 4 + 5 = _____ y _____ son _____
2. 11 + 10 = _____ y _____ son _____
3. 20 + 8 = _____ y _____ son _____
4. 16 + 2 = _____ y _____ son _____
5. 5 + 24 = _____ y _____ son _____
6. 12 + 14 = _____ y _____ son _____
7. 13 + 16 = _____ y _____ son _____
8. 27 + 2 = _____ y _____ son _____
9. 7 + 4 = _____ y _____ son _____
10. 1 + 9 = _____ y _____ son _____

Nota Gramatical   The verb **ser**   *Pupil's Edition, p. 38*

You use the verb **ser** to say where someone is from.
- To describe where you are from, you would say:
  (Yo) soy de....
- To ask a friend where he or she is from, you might say:
  ¿De dónde eres (tú)?
- To ask where someone else is from, you might say:
  ¿De dónde es Ana?

14 At an international youth conference, you overhear people telling where they're from. Fill in each blank with the correct form of **ser.**

1. Yo _____ de San Francisco, California.

2. Miguel _____ de Madrid.

3. ¿De dónde _____ tú?

4. Tú _____ de San Juan, ¿no?

5. ¿De dónde _____ Francesca?

6. Felipe _____ de Cuba.

Nota Gramatical   Forming questions   *Pupil's Edition, p. 39*

Question words are used to ask *who?, what?, where?, when?, why?,* and *how?* Examples of question words are:

¿Cómo estás? *(How are you?)*
¿Cómo te llamas? *(What's your name?* Literally, *How are you called?)*
¿Cuántos años tienes? *(How old are you?)*
¿De dónde eres? *(Where are you from?)*

15 You're transcribing some taped interviews for the school newspaper. For each of the responses below, write what the interviewer asked or said.

1. — ¿ _____?
   — Tengo quince años.

2. — ¿ _____?
   — Estoy bastante bien, gracias.

3. — ¿ _____?
   — Soy Jannie Gooden.

4. — _____
   — Soy de Managua, Nicaragua.

5. — _____
   — Me llamo Lamar Dungey.

■ TERCER PASO

To talk about what people like and don't like, you'll sometimes need to use words for various foods and pastimes.

VOCABULARIO   Foods and pastimes   *Pupil's Edition, pp. 44–45*

16 Louis is having a tough time learning the new vocabulary words. Help him by putting each word from the word box under the correct heading.

> el tenis   el jazz   la tarea   la pizza
> el baloncesto   la música clásica   el béisbol   la clase de inglés
> la fruta   la ensalada   el español   la música pop

LAS CLASES	LA COMIDA
_____	_____
_____	_____
_____	_____

LOS DEPORTES	LA MÚSICA
_____	_____
_____	_____
_____	_____

17 Several students are listing their favorite things from a specific category. Read each student's list and write the item that doesn't belong with the others.

1. _____ el béisbol   el baloncesto   la pizza
2. _____ el chocolate   el jazz   la música pop
3. _____ la fruta   la natación   la comida china
4. _____ el baloncesto   el tenis   la comida italiana
5. _____ el voleibol   la ensalada   la natación
6. _____ el tenis   el baloncesto   la tarea
7. _____ la pizza   la fruta   la música rock
8. _____ el español   la música clásica la música pop

Gramática   Nouns and definite articles   *Pupil's Edition, p. 46*

In Spanish, nouns have a <u>gender</u>—either masculine or feminine. The definite articles **el** or **la** (*the*) almost always indicate the gender of the noun. When learning a new noun, it's important to know which definite article accompanies it.

18 Complete this list of student likes and dislikes by writing the definite article that accompanies each noun.

1. _____ pizza   4. _____ español   7. _____ baloncesto

2. _____ natación   5. _____ música pop   8. _____ chocolate

3. _____ béisbol   6. _____ tenis   9. _____ fruta

19 Fill in the blanks in Ofelia's letter with the correct definite articles.

Alejandra,

¡Hola! ¿Qué tal? ¿Te gustan los deportes? Me gustan mucho. Me gustan

(1)_____ voleibol, (2)_____ natación y (3)_____

baloncesto, pero me gusta más (4)_____ tenis. Es mi favorito. También

me gusta (5)_____ música. Me gustan (6)_____ jazz y

(7)_____ música pop. Me gustan las clases, especialmente

(8)_____ clase de inglés, pero no me gusta (9)_____ tarea.

Y a ti, ¿qué te gusta hacer? ¡Chao!

Ofelia

20 Complete these statements by telling what items you like and dislike in each category. Be sure to include the definite articles in your answers.

1. *(sports)* Me gustan _____ ,

   pero no me gustan _____ .

2. *(food)* Me gustan _____ ,

   pero no me gustan _____ .

3. *(music)* Me gustan _____ ,

   pero no me gustan _____ .

4. *(school)* Me gustan _____ ,

   pero no me gustan _____ .

CAPÍTULO 2

¡Organízate!

■ PRIMER PASO

To talk about what you and others want and need, you'll need to use the words for various objects. You'll need to make nouns plural and use indefinite articles. You'll also need to understand when to use the subject pronouns **yo, tú, él,** and **ella.**

VOCABULARIO   Classroom vocabulary   *Pupil's Edition, p. 65*

1 Edward and his friends made lists of the supplies they need for school this year. First read their lists. Then complete the statements that follow to show who needs each item.

EDWARD	KHALED	JENNIFER	NORA	ETTA
una mochila	un libro	un diccionario	una mochila	una carpeta
un lápiz	una calculadora	papel	un libro	una goma
una regla	un bolígrafo	un cuaderno	una goma	de borrar
			de borrar	una regla

1. _____ needs a backpack, a pencil, and a ruler.

2. _____ needs a dictionary, paper, and a notebook.

3. _____ needs a backpack, a book, and an eraser.

4. _____ needs a book, a calculator, and a pen.

5. _____ needs a folder, an eraser, and a ruler.

2 Greg is planning to buy school supplies. Fill in the blanks with the Spanish word that best describes what he would need to . . .

1. carry his books.   _____

2. look up new words.   _____

3. organize loose papers.   _____

4. erase something.   _____

5. write notes in.   _____

6. write a draft.   _____

7. do math problems.   _____

8. measure something.   _____

Nota _G_ramatical   Indefinite articles   *Pupil's Edition, p. 66*

In Spanish, the indefinite articles **un** and **una** are the equivalent of *a* or *an*.
- **Un** is used with masculine nouns like **un cuaderno.**
- **Una** is used with feminine nouns like **una mochila.**

3 Determine the gender of the following nouns by writing them in the correct category.

MASCULINE NOUNS	FEMININE NOUNS
_____	_____
_____	_____
_____	_____
_____	_____
_____	_____

4 Several students are saying what they need for classes this year. Fill in the blanks in their statements with the correct indefinite article.

1. — Yo necesito _____ bolígrafo.

2. — Enrique necesita _____ regla para su clase de matemáticas.

3. — Liliana quiere _____ mochila.

4. — Yo quiero _____ goma de borrar.

5. — Yo quiero _____ diccionario para mi clase de español.

6. — Tú necesitas _____ carpeta, ¿no?

7. — Yo necesito _____ libro para la clase de inglés.

8. — Ya tengo _____ lápiz, pero necesito otro.

9. — Yo necesito _____ cuaderno para la clase de francés.

10. — Carlos quiere _____ calculadora para su clase de álgebra.

CAPÍTULO 2 Primer paso

Gramática   Making nouns plural   *Pupil's Edition, p. 67*

- To make a noun plural, add **-s** if it ends in a vowel: **pizza → pizzas**
- If the noun ends in a consonant, add **-es**: **pincel → pinceles**
- For nouns ending in **-z**, change **-z** to **-c** and add **-es**: **lápiz → lápices**

5 Clara picked the wrong list when she started packing for school. Correct her list by making the singular nouns (and their articles) *plural* and the plural nouns (and their articles) *singular*.

1. la mochila _____
2. el bolígrafo _____
3. el libro _____
4. la regla _____
5. la carpeta _____
6. las calculadoras _____
7. los lápices _____
8. los diccionarios _____
9. los cuadernos _____
10. las gomas de borrar _____

6 Mr. Sánchez is taking an inventory of the items in his classroom. Help him by writing the numbers with the plural forms of the nouns below.

MODELO   13 (diccionario)   **trece diccionarios**

1. 8 (carpeta) _____
2. 4 (cuaderno) _____
3. 10 (bolígrafo) _____
4. 3 (calculadora) _____
5. 20 (marcador) _____
6. 9 (lápiz) _____
7. 30 (libro) _____
8. 15 (goma de borrar) _____
9. 25 (regla) _____
10. 14 (mochila) _____

CAPÍTULO 2 Primer paso

*G*ramática   Indefinite articles   *Pupil's Edition, p. 68*

- The plural indefinite articles **unos** and **unas** mean *some* or *a few*.
- Use **unos** with a masculine plural noun. When referring to a group that includes masculine and feminine objects or males and females, the masculine plural is used.

  unos estudiantes   **unos profesores**

7 Silvia has written in her planner a list of what she needs to do tomorrow, but she has left several words out. Fill in the blanks with the correct indefinite articles.

Necesito comprar:

1. _____ calculadora y _____ regla para la clase de álgebra.
2. _____ lápices y _____ marcador para la clase de arte.
3. _____ mochila roja.
4. _____ bolígrafo para la clase de inglés.
5. _____ cuadernos y _____ carpetas para todas las clases.
6. _____ diccionario para la clase de español.
7. _____ gomas de borrar.

8 You're filling your backpack with the items you will need for your classes tomorrow. Write three items you'll put in your bag for each of the following subjects. Be sure to use indefinite articles.

1. para la clase de español: _____

   _____

2. para la clase de geometría: _____

   _____

3. para la clase de inglés: _____

   _____

4. para la clase de arte: _____

   _____

Nota *G*ramatical   Subject pronouns   *Pupil's Edition, p. 70*

- The subject pronoun **yo** *(I)* is used when you're talking about yourself and **tú** *(you)* is used when you're talking to a friend.

    Yo necesito tres carpetas. **Tú** necesitas dos cuadernos, ¿verdad?

- The subject pronouns **él** *(he)* or **ella** *(she)* are used when you're talking about someone else.

    Manuel y Sara son mis amigos. **Él** es del Perú. **Ella** es de Chile.

- In Spanish, subject pronouns are used mainly for clarity or emphasis, since the verb shows who the subject of the sentence is.

9 Your teacher has asked Mónica to walk around the room and introduce herself and others. Fill in the blanks with the correct subject pronoun.

1. _____ soy Mónica Buendía.

2. _____ es Juan Pablo Sánchez.

3. _____ eres Gregorio, ¿no?

4. _____ es Melissa Johnson.

5. _____ es una amiga.

10 Margaret is just learning how to work with subject pronouns. Which pronoun would she use when . . . ?

_____ 1. describing herself

_____ 2. describing a male classmate

_____ 3. talking to a friend

_____ 4. describing a female neighbor

_____ 5. describing your male cousin

_____ 6. talking about your friend's mother

_____ 7. talking to her best friend

_____ 8. describing your uncle

_____ 9. telling someone where she's from

_____ 10. telling someone how old she is

CAPÍTULO 2 Primer paso

■ SEGUNDO PASO

To describe the contents of your room, you'll need to use the appropriate vocabulary. You'll also need to use the adjectives **mucho** and **cuánto**.

VOCABULARIO   Bedroom vocabulary   *Pupil's Edition, p. 75*

11 Lily has a summer job working in a hotel in Santo Domingo. It's her responsibility to inventory the rooms periodically to be sure all of the furniture is there. Combine the elements given to say how many of each items are in the room. You may want to use the words in the word box. Use **hay** in your sentences.

lámpara	escritorio	cama	silla	reloj
revista	mesa	ventana	cartel	radio	armario

MODELO   3 / posters   **Hay tres carteles.**

1. 2 / beds

   _____

2. 1 / closet

   _____

3. 3 / lamps

   _____

4. 4 / chairs

   _____

5. 1 / table

   _____

6. 1 / clock

   _____

7. 1 / desk

   _____

12 In the blank provided, write the item that doesn't belong with the others.

1. _____   ventana   escritorio   puerta

2. _____   escritorio   mesa   radio

3. _____   zapatilla de tenis   revista   libro

4. _____   reloj   cartel   mesa

5. _____   radio   televisor   armario

¡Ven conmigo! Adelante Level 1A, Chapter 2

*G*ramática   Agreement of **mucho** and **cuánto**   *Pupil's Edition, p. 78*

- In Spanish, many adjectives have endings that change depending on whether the noun is masculine or feminine (agreement in gender), singular or plural (agreement in number). These changes are shown in the following chart:

	Singular	Plural
Masculine	bueno	buenos
Feminine	buena	buenas

- Various forms of **¿cuánto?** are used to ask *how much?* or *how many?* **¿Cuánto?** is an adjective, so it agrees with the noun it is describing.

  ¿Cuánto papel necesitas?   **¿Cuánta** tarea tienes?

  ¿Cuántos libros hay?   **¿Cuántas** carpetas quieres?

- The adjective **mucho** *(a lot, much, many)* also agrees in number and gender.

	Singular	Plural
Masculine	mucho	muchos
Feminine	mucha	muchas

  Hay **muchos** libros, **muchas** mochilas y **mucho** papel.

  Tengo **mucha** tarea para la clase de español.

13 You're taking a survey to find out what things your classmates have in their rooms. Read the following sentences or questions and fill in the blanks with the correct form of **cuánto** or **mucho**.

1. ¿_____ carteles hay en tu cuarto? (cuánto)

2. ¿_____ revistas hay? (cuánto)

3. ¿_____ gomas de borrar hay en el escritorio? (cuánto)

4. ¿_____ lápices hay? (cuánto)

5. ¿_____ ventanas hay en tu cuarto? (cuánto)

Now, you're announcing some of the results of your survey. Fill in the blanks with the correct form of **mucho**.

6. Tengo _____ bolígrafos. (mucho)

7. Necesito _____ cuadernos. (mucho)

8. Hay _____ ropa en el armario. (mucho)

9. Mónica tiene _____ sillas en su cuarto. (mucho)

10. Luis tiene _____ zapatillas de tenis. (mucho)

11. Raúl necesita _____ gomas de borrar. (mucho)

■ TERCER PASO

CAPÍTULO 2 Tercer paso

To talk about what you need and want to do, you'll need to use infinitives. You'll also need to use numbers from 31 to 199.

VOCABULARIO   Expressions with **necesitar** and **querer**   *Pupil's Edition, p. 86*

14 Silvia and Mario are talking about what they have to do or want to do this weekend. Fill in the blanks with the verbs in the word box. Some of the verbs will be used more than once.

> comprar   conocer   encontrar   poner   ir

SILVIA   Yo necesito **(1)** _____ mis cosas en el armario. Mi cuarto está

muy desorganizado. También, quiero **(2)** _____ mi dinero.

Necesito **(3)** _____ el libro para la clase de inglés.

MARIO   Bueno, yo quiero **(4)** _____ al centro comercial. Si quieres,

podemos *(we can)* **(5)** _____ juntos.

SILVIA   Buena idea. Pero tengo que **(6)** _____ a Linda y Michael en la

plaza a las cinco. ¿Quieres **(7)** _____ a mis amigos?

MARIO   Sí. ¡Vamos a la plaza a las cinco!

Nota *G*ramatical   Infinitives   *Pupil's Edition, p. 86*

Verbs like **comprar** *(to buy)*, **poner** *(to put)*, **conocer** *(to know, to meet)*, and **ir** *(to go)*, are called <u>infinitives</u>.

- In English, infinitives begin with the word *to: to run, to walk, to live.* In Spanish, infinitives always end with -**ar**, -**er**, or -**ir** (**organizar, hacer, escribir**).

---

15 Read what each person does before the school year starts and fill in the blanks with the correct infinitive from the choices given. You may use the infinitives more than once.

> ir   conocer   comprar   poner

TOMÁS   Yo necesito **(1)**_____ muchos carteles para mi cuarto.

HAN-LING   Dana quiere **(2)**_____ a unos nuevos amigos.

KERRI   Teresa necesita **(3)**_____ unos cuadernos.

SABINA   Tú necesitas **(4)**_____ los libros en la mochila, ¿no?

WILL   ¿Quieres **(5)**_____ al centro comercial hoy *(today)*?

VOCABULARIO   Numbers from 31 to 199   *Pupil's Edition, p. 88*

16 When you're in a Spanish-speaking country, you'll often hear telephone numbers spoken in pairs. Match the telephone numbers on the left with the corresponding words on the right.

_____ 1. 31-42-65

_____ 2. 79-33-98

_____ 3. 6-44-46-82

_____ 4. 86-72-60

_____ 5. 54-91-50

_____ 6. 6-39-48-99

_____ 7. 70-92-47

_____ 8. 61-80-75

_____ 9. 5-42-14-02

_____ 10. 54-91-15

_____ 11. 5-42-40-13

_____ 12. 86-72-66

a. setenta y nueve, treinta y tres, noventa y ocho

b. ochenta y seis, sesenta y dos, setenta

c. setenta, noventa y dos, cuarenta y siete

d. cincuenta y cuatro, noventa y uno, cincuenta

e. treinta y uno, cuarenta y dos, sesenta y cinco

f. sesenta y uno, ochenta, setenta y cinco

g. seis, treinta y nueve, cuarenta y ocho, noventa y nueve

h. treinta y uno, cincuenta y seis, sesenta y cinco

i. cuarenta y seis, noventa y tres, ochenta y cuatro

j. ochenta y seis, setenta y dos, sesenta

k. seis, cuarenta y cuatro, cuarenta y seis, ochenta y dos

l. ochenta y seis, setenta y dos, sesenta y seis

m. cinco, cuarenta y dos, cuarenta, trece

n. cincuenta y cuatro, noventa y uno, quince

o. cinco, cuarenta y dos, catorce, cero dos

17 You're helping your parents shop for items to refurnish your room. Write how much money you need to buy the following items.

MODELO   un reloj ($32)   **treinta y dos dólares**

1. un televisor ($198) _____ dólares

2. una radio ($50) _____ dólares

3. un armario ($199) _____ dólares

4. un teléfono ($60) _____ dólares

5. un reloj ($15) _____ dólares

6. una mesa ($75) _____ dólares

7. una lámpara ($46) _____ dólares

8. una silla ($80) _____ dólares

9. un escritorio ($185) _____ dólares

10. dos carteles ($36) _____ dólares

11. una cama ($199) _____ dólares

CAPÍTULO 3

Nuevas clases, nuevos amigos

■ PRIMER PASO

To talk about class schedules and to sequence events, you'll need to use the names of academic subjects. To tell time, you'll need to use numbers and some forms of the verb **ser**.

VOCABULARIO　　　Academic subjects　　*Pupil's Edition, p. 109*

1 Ms. Sosa is a new advisor at school and she's helping students choose their classes for next semester. Based on each student's interests, write two classes that he or she might enjoy.

las matemáticas	**el arte**	**la geografía**	**las ciencias**
la educación física	**la computación**	**el francés**	**las ciencias sociales**

1. Mauricio enjoys sculpting, painting, and learning foreign languages.

   _____ y _____

2. Melinda likes computers and working with numbers.

   _____ y _____

3. Becky enjoys playing softball and wants to be a veterinarian.

   _____ y _____

4. Teodoro likes drawing and finding out about different countries.

   _____ y _____

5. Laura likes learning about society and would like to be an accountant.

   _____ y _____

2 Agnes has chicken pox, so her friend Julie is picking up this week's assignments for her. Julie forgot to write the subjects for each of the assignments. Help Agnes figure out which class each assignment is for.

1. pintar un autorretrato *(self-portrait)* _____

2. dibujar un mapa de España _____

3. leer el poema *"Chanson de Jacques et son chat Marcel"* _____

4. memorizar las tablas de multiplicar _____

5. estudiar el sistema de respiración _____

Nota _G_ramatical Plural definite articles *Pupil's Edition, p. 109*

- For the word *the*, use **los** with plural masculine nouns.
  - **los** lib**ros**, **los** cuadern**os**, **los** amig**os**
- Use **las** with plural feminine nouns.
  - **las** cam**as**, **las** lámpar**as**, **las** amig**as**

3 Mr. Gómez is taking an inventory of supplies to distribute to his students for the new school year. Write the correct definite article for each item he has for his students.

1. _____ cuadernos   6. _____ lápices

2. _____ gomas de borrar   7. _____ reglas

3. _____ diccionario   8. _____ libros

4. _____ carpetas   9. _____ calculadoras

5. _____ revistas   10. _____ bolígrafos

4 Jeff has just taken a job as a waiter at Ana's Pizzeria. Fill in the blanks with the correct definite articles to complete his paragraph about the items he finds there.

A ver... en (1) _____ pizzería hay muchas cosas. (2) _____ sillas y (3) _____

mesas son para todos (4) _____ clientes que están en el restaurante. (5) _____ comida

italiana, (6) _____ ensaladas y (7) _____ pizzas son muy populares. También

(8) _____ chocolate y (9) _____ frutas son muy deliciosos.

5 Read the following dialogues and fill in the blanks with the correct definite articles.

MAMÁ ¿Qué quieres para (1) _____ clases este semestre?

JUANITO Bueno, Mamá, quiero (2) _____ zapatillas de tenis que están de moda *(in style)*.

* * *

ABUELA ¿Tienes (3) _____ cosas que te compré *(I bought for you)* en tu mochila?

ISABEL Sí. Tengo (4) _____ cuadernos, (5) _____

bolígrafos, (6) _____ diccionario y (7) _____ calculadora.

* * *

PROFESOR ¿Dónde están (8) _____ libros?

GRACIELA Tengo (9) _____ libros y (10) _____ revistas en mi escritorio, Profesor Sánchez.

*G*ramática   Telling time   *Pupil's Edition, p. 113*

- To tell the time, use **Son las...** plus the hour.

    Son las dos.   **Son las** cuatro.   **Son las** diez.

- After the hour, add the minutes with the word **y** *(and)*.

    Son las seis **y diez.**   Son las siete **y media.**   Son las once **y cuarto.**

- After the half hour, subtract the minutes to the next hour with the word **menos** *(minus)*.

    Son las cinco **menos veinte.**

    Son las tres **menos cuarto.**

- For times including one o'clock, use **Es la...**

    Es la una.   **Es la** una y veinte.

6 Valerie is spending Saturday afternoon working in her grandmother's clock store. Her task is to set the correct time on a shipment of new clocks. In Spanish, help Valerie catalog the new shipment by matching each clock to the correct time.

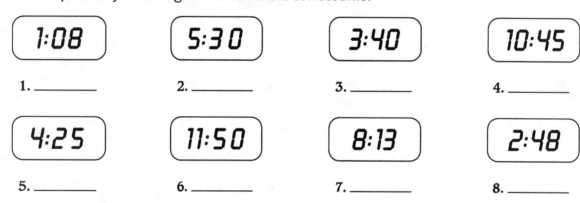

1:08   5:30   3:40   10:45

1. _____   2. _____   3. _____   4. _____

4:25   11:50   8:13   2:48

5. _____   6. _____   7. _____   8. _____

a. Son las doce menos diez.   **f.** Es la una y ocho.

b. Son las cuatro menos veinte.   **g.** Son las cuatro y veinticinco.

c. Son las tres menos doce.   **h.** Son las cinco y media.

d. Son las ocho y trece.   **i.** Es la una y media.

e. Son las once menos cuarto.

7 Fernando, a radio disk jockey for a Spanish radio station in Baltimore, frequently announces the time during his shift. Write the following times he says one afternoon.

1. 12:35 _____

2. 2:04 _____

3. 2:50 _____

4. 3:20 _____

5. 4:00 _____

6. 5:30 _____

CAPÍTULO 3 Primer paso

20 Grammar and Vocabulary Workbook   ¡Ven conmigo! Adelante Level 1A, Chapter 3

■ SEGUNDO PASO

To tell at what time something happens, you'll need to respond to the question
¿A qué hora...?

VOCABULARIO   Time expressions   *Pupil's Edition, p. 119*

8 Germán programmed the computers at the airport with arrival times from particular cities. For each of the times listed below, write what the computer will display.

MODELO   *Nashville* - 3:46 A.M.   **A las cuatro menos catorce de la mañana.**

1. *St. Louis* - 7:40 A.M. _____

2. *Chicago* - 7:30 A.M. _____

3. *Des Moines* - 6:15 A.M. _____

4. *Gary* - 8:50 P.M. _____

5. *Detroit* - 11:25 P.M. _____

6. *Toledo* - 4:55 A.M. _____

7. *Madison* - 3:13 P.M. _____

8. *Dubuque* - 12:30 P.M. _____

9 Abby has just received her schedule for the new semester. Use the schedule to help her figure out what class she has today at each time listed below.

8:30 - 9:15	la computación
9:20 - 10:05	el arte
10:10 - 10:55	las matemáticas
11:00 - 11:45	las ciencias
11:50 - 12:30	el descanso
12:35 - 1:20	la educación física
1:25 - 2:10	la geografía
2:15 - 3:00	las ciencias sociales

MODELO   Abby tiene la clase de arte **a las diez menos cinco.**

1. Abby tiene la clase de educación física _____.

2. Abby tiene la clase de ciencias _____.

3. Abby tiene la clase de ciencias sociales _____.

4. Abby tiene la clase de geografía _____.

5. Abby tiene la clase de matemáticas _____.

6. Abby tiene la clase de arte _____.

CAPÍTULO 3 Segundo paso

Nota Gramatical   Possession using de   *Pupil's Edition, p. 121*

To show possession in Spanish, use **de.** This is the equivalent of *-'s* (apostrophe *s*) in English.

los cuadernos de Eva   *Eva's notebooks*
la mochila de Pablo   *Paul's backpack*
el libro de Anita y Eduardo   *Anita and Edward's book*
los lápices de Carlos y Felipe   *Carlos and Felipe's pencils*

10 Chris and her brother Bob have just moved into their new home. Write the following items they have unpacked.

MODELO   lamp / Chris   **la lámpara de Chris**

1. posters / Bob _____

2. tennis shoes / Chris _____

3. clothing / Bob _____

4. radio / Chris _____

5. table / Bob _____

6. magazines / Chris _____

7. TV set / Bob _____

8. clock / Chris _____

9. chair / Bob _____

11 It's a busy Monday morning for Mr. Contreras! The dining room table is covered with his children's school supplies and he's trying to figure out what items belong to which child. Follow the model to help him out.

MODELO   Silvia's folders   **Las carpetas son de Silvia.**

1. Eduardo and Lupe's books _____

2. Silvia's pens _____

3. Lupe and Eduardo's pencils _____

4. Lupe's erasers _____

5. Eduardo's ruler _____

6. Silvia's backpack _____

7. Lupe's dictionary_____

8. Silvia and Eduardo's papers _____

9. Silvia's notebooks _____

¡Ven conmigo! Adelante Level 1A, Chapter 3

CAPÍTULO 3 Segundo paso

■ TERCER PASO

To describe people and things, you'll need to use the verb **ser** and adjectives. To talk about things you like and explain why, you'll need to use the verb **gustar**.

Nota Gramatical   The verb **ser**   *Pupil's Edition, p. 126*

The verb **ser** *(to be)* is an irregular verb. It conjugates as follows:

yo **soy**	nosotros **somos**
tú **eres**	vosotros sois
él, ella, Ud. **es**	ellos, ellas, Uds. **son**

---

12 Bobby has written a note to Marco, his pen pal in Bolivia, about himself and his friends. Complete his note with the correct forms of the verb **ser.**

¡Hola Marco!

Me llamo Bobby y (1) _____ de Portland, Oregon.

Yo (2) _____ inteligente y bajo. También

(3) _____ guapo y un poco cómico. ¿Y mis amigos?

Bueno, ellos (4) _____ amigos muy buenos. Una amiga

(5) _____ Cindy. Ella (6) _____

muy bonita. Otro amigo, Louis, (7) _____ muy

divertido. Cindy y Louis (8) _____ muy simpáticos.

Nosotros (9) _____ muy buenos amigos. Y, ¿cómo

(10) _____ tú?

Tu amigo, Bobby

13 Answer the following questions about yourself and your friends in complete sentences.

1. ¿De dónde eres? _____

2. ¿De dónde es tu profesor(a) de español? _____

3. ¿Cómo eres? _____

4. ¿Cómo es tu mejor(a) amigo(a)? _____

5. ¿De dónde son tus padres? _____

VOCABULARIO   Adjectives   *Pupil's Edition, p. 125*

14 Rosa is describing some famous people and characters to her best friend Dena, but Dena can't figure out who is who! Help her out by matching the description on the left with the correct person or character on the right.

1. _____ Son morenos y muy guapos.

2. _____ Es muy alto y feo.

3. _____ Es morena, baja y bonita.

4. _____ Son rubias y bonitas.

5. _____ Son muy inteligentes.

6. _____ Es guapo y rubio.

a. Brad Pitt

b. Claudia Schiffer y Heather Locklear

c. Frankenstein

d. Gloria Estefan

e. Antonio Banderas y Andy García

f. Albert Einstein y Marie Curie

15 Fernando is describing some of his friends to his grandfather. Help him out by creating sentences using the cues provided.

MODELO   Clara (cómico)   **Clara es cómica.**

1. Juan y Pepe (alto) _____

2. Eva (bajo y bonito) _____

3. Silvia y Laura (inteligente) _____

4. Pablo y Teodoro (guapo y rubio) _____

   _____

5. Diana y Carlos (divertido y simpático) _____

   _____

16 Now it's your turn! Describe each of the following people with three adjectives from the **Vocabulario** box on page 125 of your textbook.

MODELO   Mi profesora favorita **es la señora Dakhlia. Ella es inteligente, cómica y muy simpática.**

1. Mi profesor favorito _____ .

   _____ .

2. Mi actriz favorita _____ .

   _____ .

3. Mi actor favorito _____ .

   _____ .

4. Mi clase favorita _____ .

   _____ .

Gramática   Adjective agreement   *Pupil's Edition, p. 127*

- Adjectives change to match the number and gender of the nouns they modify.

	Masculine	Feminine
Singular	un amig**o** cómic**o**	un**a** amig**a** cómic**a**
Plural	un**os** amig**os** cómic**os**	un**as** amig**as** cómic**as**

- When describing a group of females and males, use a masculine plural adjective.

  Eva y Juan son **antipáticos.**

- Adjectives ending in **-e** or a consonant don't match in gender, but they match in number.

  El amigo es **inteligente.** → Los amigos son **inteligentes.**
  La clase es **interesante.** → Las clases son **interesantes.**

17 Dena has now made a list of famous people with Rosa's help. Can you create sentences using the adjectives supplied for the people on her list?

1. Winona Ryder / ser / bajo y simpático

   _____

2. Bill Cosby / ser / inteligente y cómico

   _____

3. Alicia Silverstone / ser / rubio y cómico

   _____

4. Danny Devito / ser / divertido y bajo

   _____

5. Michelle Pfeiffer y Rachel Hunter / ser / rubio y bonito

   _____

6. Daniel Day-Lewis / ser / alto y delgado

   _____

7. Tom Hanks y Robin Williams / ser / bajo y guapo

   _____

8. Shaquille O'Neal y Michael Jordan / ser / alto y simpático

   _____

9. Queen Latifah y Billy Crystal / ser / inteligente y divertido

   _____

10. Tom Cruise y Demi Moore / ser / inteligente y guapo

    _____

CAPÍTULO 3 Tercer paso

VOCABULARIO   Pastime words   *Pupil's Edition, p. 130*

18 Several friends are talking about things they like. Fill in the blanks with the best word from the word box.

```
fiestas        partido      videojuegos      deportes
      bailes         novela        concierto      examen
```

MANUEL   ¿Te gusta bailar?

ANGÉLICA   Sí, mis **(1)** _____ favoritos son la salsa y el merengue.

* * *

LUIS   ¿Cuáles son tus **(2)** _____ favoritos?

ESTEBAN   Me gusta el tenis, el voleibol y el béisbol.

* * *

ANTONIA   ¿Te gusta la literatura?

ARTURO   Sí, mi **(3)** _____ favorita es *Cien años de soledad.*

* * *

STEPHANIE   ¿Te gusta la música rock?

JULIO   Sí, me encanta.

STEPHANIE   ¿Quieres ir al **(4)** _____ de música conmigo?

* * *

GABRIEL   Me gustan mucho las **(5)** _____ .

MARISOL   ¿Por qué?

GABRIEL   Porque allí puedes bailar, escuchar música y celebrar con tus amigos.

19 Unscramble the letters in the boxes to reveal the correct pastime for each of the following sentences. Then write your answer in the blank provided.

1. A Julieta le gustan las I S F E A T S de Navidad *(Christmas).* _____

2. Me gustan los I E L S B A porque me encanta la música. _____

3. ¿Te gusta leer V A S N E O L o revistas? _____

4. Me gustan los S C E N O R I O T C de música latina. _____

5. A Juanita no le gustan los D A T I P S O R de béisbol. _____

CAPÍTULO

4 ¿Qué haces esta tarde?

■ PRIMER PASO

To talk about what you like to do during your free time, you'll need to use the present tense. You'll also need to use the words **con** *(with)* and **que** *(that, which, or who)* to say with whom you do these activities.

VOCABULARIO   Activities around the house   *Pupil's Edition, p. 149*

1 Jamila and several friends are discussing what they like to do on weekends. Choose the infinitive from the word box that best completes each sentence.

lavar	cuidar	nadar
escuchar	descansar	
mirar	dibujar	pintar	sacar

JAMILA   A mí me gusta (1) _____ la televisión.

ANDRÉS   Me gusta (2) _____ en el parque.

JULIO   A mí me gusta el parque también. Especialmente me gusta

(3) _____ en la piscina.

LEN   A mí me gusta (4) _____ música.

ELI   Berta, te gusta el arte, ¿verdad? ¿Te gusta (5) _____?

BERTA   Sí, a mí me gusta dibujar y (6) _____ .

RAÚL   Me gusta (7) _____ el carro de mis padres.

2 Now, Jamila's friends are talking about what they need to do this weekend. Fill in each blank with an appropriate verb from the box in Activity 1.

ELI   Jamila, necesitas (1) _____ a tu hermano también, ¿no?

LEN   Yo necesito (2) _____ la basura.

JULIO   Quiero (3) _____ la ropa.

ANDRÉS   Necesito (4) _____ el carro.

JAMILA   Yo quiero (5) _____ para mi clase de arte.

BERTA   Necesito (6) _____ un programa de televisión para la clase de historia.

RAÚL   Necesito (7) _____ al gato *(cat)*.

Gramática   Present tense of regular -ar verbs   *Pupil's Edition, p. 150*

- In Spanish and English, you have to change verbs according to their subjects. This is called *conjugating* the verb.
- To conjugate a regular -**ar** verb, such as **nadar,** drop the -**ar** from the infinitive and add one of the following endings to the stem:

nadar → nad-

(yo) -**o** → nad**o** *I swim*	(nosotros) -**amos** → nad**amos** *we swim*	
(tú) -**as** → nad**as** *you swim*	(vosotros) -áis → nadáis *you* (pl., Spain) *swim*	
(él, ella, usted) -**a** → nad**a** *he/ she/ you swim(s)*	(ellos, ellas, ustedes) -**an** → nad**an** *you* (pl.) *swim, they swim*	

3 Alma is working as a counselor at summer camp. She has written a list of what some campers are doing there. Fill in the blanks with the correct forms of the verbs given in parentheses.

... Perla (1) _____ (tocar) la guitarra.

Cristina y Jorge (2) _____ (practicar)

deportes. Renaldo (3) _____ (dibujar).

Tyrone (4) _____ (escuchar) música.

Rafael y Theo (5) _____ (descansar).

Nora (6) _____ (lavar) la ropa.

René (7) _____ (hablar) por teléfono ...

4 Alma's mother has just received the above letter and is going to write a response. Help her write a letter to Alma by forming sentences using the elements below.

MODELO   Harry / hablar con sus amigos   **Harry habla con sus amigos.**

1. Miguel / estudiar / todos los días

_____

2. Rosita y Daphne / cantar en el coro *(choir)*

_____

3. Yo / no / bailar mucho

_____

4. Nosotros / mirar / la televisión / bastante

_____

5 In the letter that Alma's parents are writing, they also want to ask her what activities she and her new friends are doing. Use the following fragments to write questions.

MODELO   Luis / hablar mucho por teléfono   **¿Habla Luis mucho por teléfono?**

1. Tus amigas / escuchar música

   ¿ _____?

2. Tú / nadar en la piscina

   ¿ _____?

3. Tú y tus amigos / lavar los platos

   ¿ _____?

4. Tú / sacar la basura / todos los días

   ¿ _____?

6 Write four sentences about yourself and your friends and family.

1. (yo) hablar por teléfono _____

2. (mis amigos) nadar _____

3. (mi papá) sacar la basura _____

4. (mi famila y yo) mirar la televisión _____

   _____

VOCABULARIO   Pastime activities   *Pupil's Edition, p. 154*

7 Tanya has made a list of the things she plans to do today. Complete the statements and then circle the activities that she planned to do on the following puzzle. The verbs will be in the infinitive form.

1. _____ con el perro

2. _____ el rato con amigos

3. _____ en bicicleta

4. _____ la cena

5. _____ un refresco

6. _____ la guitarra

```
P  A  T  C  A  M  B  Y  Y  B  K
H  I  D  O  T  X  A  H  E  Z  H
D  A  N  A  M  D  V  N  M  O  A
U  F  I  D  A  A  D  Z  E  Q  L
T  R  P  A  S  A  R  S  N  A  E
H  A  R  B  K  P  A  U  I  L  D
B  F  E  H  T  E  R  R  C  I  J
T  H  P  L  M  O  N  T  A  R  E
R  C  A  I  K  E  R  R  M  O  N
A  H  R  D  N  M  K  L  I  P  N
B  E  A  E  B  R  X  Z  N  O  I
A  D  R  N  A  S  F  D  A  I  H
J  L  T  N  T  O  C  A  R  L  I
A  I  E  S  W  E  R  T  Y  U  C
R  C  W  E  M  E  H  C  I  H  H
```

Nota Gramatical   The preposition con   *Pupil's Edition, p. 155*

- Use **con** *(with)* + the pronouns you've already learned for *him, her, them, us,* and *you* (pl.):

   Ana y Eva estudian con **nosotros.** Luis estudia con **ustedes.** Marta estudia con Pepe, y Tomás estudia con **ellos** también.

- The following expressions mean *with me* and *with you*:

   Yo practico deportes **contigo** *(with you)* y tú escuchas música **conmigo** *(with me)*. ¿De acuerdo?

8 Nora works in a dance studio. Help her direct her dancers by filling in the blanks with the correct expressions with **con.** Replace the names in parentheses with subject pronouns.

MODELO   Lorenzo baila **con ella.** (Annette).

1. Rosario baila _____ (Julio y yo).

2. Susana baila _____ (Jesús)

3. Natalia baila _____ (tú).

4. Alejandro baila _____ (Elizabeth).

5. Ignacio baila _____ (Paloma y Ana).

6. Mario baila _____ (yo).

Nota Gramatical   The word que   *Pupil's Edition, p. 157*

The word **que,** used to refer to people or things, means *that, which,* or *who.*
   Tengo una amiga **que** habla español. *I have a friend <u>who</u> speaks Spanish.*
   La comida **que** me gusta comer es pizza. *The food <u>that</u> I like to eat is pizza.*

9 Write four sentences using the fragments below.

COLUMN A	COLUMN B	COLUMN C
el chico	tocar el piano	Luisa
la chica	nadar en la piscina	Nicolás
la profesora	dibujar	el señor González
el profesor	estudiar	la señora Ramos
	montar en bicicleta	

1. _____

2. _____

3. _____

4. _____

■ SEGUNDO PASO

To talk about where people or things are, you'll need to use the verb **estar**, places in town, and prepositions of location. You'll also need to use the subject pronouns for clarity or emphasis.

> Nota **G**ramatical   The present tense of **estar**   *Pupil's Edition, p. 162*
>
> The verb **estar** is used to talk about where things or people are located.
>
> (Yo) **estoy** en la farmacia.   (Nosotros, nosotras) **estamos** en el cuarto.
> (Tú) **estás** en el parque.   (Vosotros, vosotras) **estáis** en la clase.
> (Él) **está** en la piscina.   (Ellos or Ellas) **están** en la pizzería.
> (Ella) **está** en la piscina.   (Ustedes) **están** en la pizzería.
> (Usted) **está** en la piscina.

10 Taci's friend Beverly has been living in another state for the last year. Beverly has returned for the weekend and has many questions about where people and things are. Help Taci answer Beverly's questions by filling in the blanks with the correct forms of **estar.**

BEVERLY   ¿Dónde **(1)** _____ Joan?

TACI   Ella **(2)** _____ en Cincinnati con su abuela.

BEVERLY   ¿Y Lonnie?

TACI   Él **(3)** _____ en la biblioteca.

BEVERLY   ¿Y Rolando y Tomás?

TACI   **(4)** _____ en el trabajo.

BEVERLY   ¿Y Paquito?

TACI   **(5)** _____ en su casa.

BEVERLY   ¿Y Freddy y Cindy?

TACI   **(6)** _____ en el centro.

BEVERLY   ¿Y dónde **(7)** _____ tú y tu familia?

TACI   **(8)** _____ en una casa en la calle Bolívar.

11 Write a sentence telling where each of the following people is now:

1. yo _____

2. mi mejor amigo(a) _____

_____

3. El Presidente de los Estados Unidos_____

_____

4. Mis papás *(parents)* _____

| **VOCABULARIO** | Places and prepositions of location | *Pupil's Edition, p. 163* |

12 Help Lois solve the following riddles. Fill in the first blank with the correct form of the verb in parentheses and the second blank with the place where this would be likely to occur.

---

el gimnasio

el supermercado   el correo

la biblioteca   la tienda   el parque   la piscina

el cine

MODELO   Cristóbal _____ (descansar) en _____ .
         Cristóbal **descansa** en **el parque.**

1. Rodolfo y Berta _____ (comprar) la comida en _____ .

2. Sally _____ (nadar) en _____ .

3. Tú _____ (comprar) ropa en _____ .

4. Nosotros _____ (estudiar) para los exámenes en _____ .

5. Me gusta _____ (ver) películas en _____ .

6. Ustedes _____ (practicar) deportes en _____ .

7. Yo _____ (necesitar) comprar estampillas en _____ .

13 Aiyana has just moved to San Juan, Puerto Rico. Use the items in the word box to help her find her way around by telling where things are located according to the diagram below.

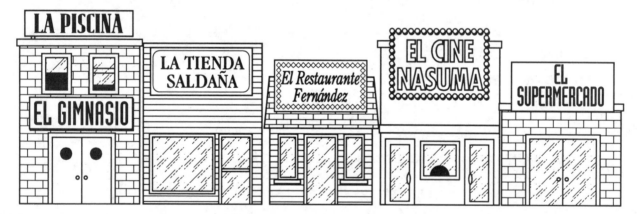

1. El Cine Nasuma está _____ del supermercado.

2. El supermercado está _____ del gimnasio.

3. La piscina está _____ del gimnasio.

4. La Tienda Saldaña está _____ del restaurante.

5. El gimnasio está _____ de la piscina.

al lado   debajo

               encima

cerca

        lejos

*G*ramática   Subject pronouns   *Pupil's Edition, p. 166*

- The subject pronouns in Spanish are:

yo *(I)*	**nosotros / nosotras** *(we)*
tú *(you)*	**vosotros / vosotras** *(you)* (pl., Spain)
él *(he or it)*	**ellos** *(they)*
ella *(she or it)*	**ellas** *(they)*
usted *(you)* (formal)	**ustedes** *(you)* (pl.)

- **Usted** (abbreviated **Ud.**) and **tú** both mean *you*. Use **tú** (the familiar *you*) when talking to a friend, a family member, or someone your own age or younger. Use **usted** (the formal *you*) when talking to an adult who isn't a family member. In Latin America, *you* (pl.) is always **ustedes**.

- **Ellos** and **ellas** both mean *they*. Use **ellas** when you're talking about a group of females. Use **ellos** if you're talking about a group of males or a group of males and females together.

14 The following statements tell what you and your classmates do. Rewrite the statements by replacing the underlined portion with the correct subject pronoun.

MODELO   <u>Vicky</u> quiere nadar. → **<u>Ella</u>** quiere nadar.

1. <u>Robert y Jeremy</u> preparan la cena. _____

2. <u>Tabitha y Janie</u> miran la televisión. _____

3. <u>Todd y Felicia</u> nadan en la piscina. _____

4. <u>Nancy</u> camina con el perro. _____

5. <u>Jerome</u> toma un helado. _____

6. <u>Mario y yo</u> necesitamos trabajar. _____

15 Would you use **tú** or **usted** to address these people?

1. tu amigo Samuel _____

2. tu profesor de inglés _____

3. la madre de tu amiga _____

4. tu profesora de francés _____

5. tu amiga Mavis _____

6. tu papá _____

16 How would you . . . ?

1. ask the principal of your school how she or he is

   ¿ _____ ?

2. tell your younger sister that she talks a lot on the telephone

   _____ .

3. ask your friend Juan if he watches television

   ¿ _____ ?

4. ask your Spanish teacher if he or she plays the piano

   ¿ _____ ?

■ TERCER PASO

To talk about where you and others go during free time, you'll need to use the verb **ir** and the days of the week with definite articles.

> ## Nota *G*ramatical   The verb **ir**   *Pupil's Edition, p. 172*
>
> The verb **ir** *(to go)* is conjugated as follows:
>
> | | |
> |---|---|
> | yo **voy** | nosotros **vamos** |
> | tú **vas** | vosotros vais |
> | él, ella, Ud. **va** | ellos, ellas, Uds. **van** |

17 Several of Adolfo's friends are going on vacation. Fill in the blanks with the correct form of **ir** to say where he and his friends are going.

1. Alicia y yo _____ a Inglaterra.

2. Y luego yo _____ a España.

3. Pablo _____ a Japón.

4. Norma, tú _____ a Perú, ¿no?

5. Arlon y Félix _____ a Bolivia.

6. Nannette y Silvia _____ a Rusia.

7. Señora, usted _____ a Australia, ¿no?

8. Ustedes _____ a Argentina, ¿verdad?

18 All of your friends are going somewhere this weekend. Combine words and phrases from all three columns to say where they are going.

COLUMN A		COLUMN B
Priscilla		al centro
Juan Carlos		a la biblioteca
Yo		al cine
Tú	+ IR +	a la ciudad
Usted		al restaurante
Ustedes		a la piscina
Eva y yo		al parque
Bruce y Franklin		al gimnasio

MODELO   **Priscilla va al restaurante.**

1. _____

2. _____

3. _____

4. _____

5. _____

6. _____

7. _____

VOCABULARIO   Days of the week   *Pupil's Edition, p. 174*

19 Cindy has been very busy lately. Look at her schedule and answer the questions about when she is going to do different activities.

lunes	martes	miércoles	jueves	viernes	sábado	domingo
ir a un concierto con Manuel	nadar en la piscina de Mónica	ir al cine con Corey y Elena	estudiar en la biblioteca	ir al restaurante con mis papás	montar en bicicleta en el parque	jugar al tenis con Felipe

1. ¿Cuándo *(When)* va a escuchar música? _____

2. ¿Cuándo va a hacer ejercicio? _____ , _____

   y _____

3. ¿Cuándo va a ver una película? _____

4. ¿Cuándo va a comer con sus papás? _____

5. ¿Cuándo va a estudiar? _____

20 On the following calendar, write the names of the weekdays and what you're planning to do for each day. Use the following guidelines: Mondays are exercise days, Tuesdays are outdoor days, Wednesdays are study days, Thursdays are work days and Fridays are days to be with friends. The first entry has been done for you.

montar en bicicleta   descansar en el parque   nadar   bailar con mis amigos

trabajar

mirar la televisión   cantar   ir a la biblioteca   pasar el rato con amigos

lunes				
nadar con mis amigos				

Nota Gramatical   Expressions with days of the week   *Pupil's Edition, p. 174*

- To say that you do something on a particular day, use **el** + the day of the week.

  El viernes voy al cine con Mathilde.
  On Friday, I'm going to the movies with Mathilde.

- To say that you do something regularly on a certain day, use **los** + the day.

  Los viernes ceno con mis papás.
  On Fridays, I have dinner with my parents.

- You do not use **el** or **los** before the day when you say what day of the week it is.

  Hoy es lunes. *Today is Monday.*

- The days of the week are not capitalized in Spanish text.

21 For these sentences, decide whether the event is taking place **(O)** once on a particular day, **(R)** regularly on a certain day, or **(D)** if the statement is telling what day it is today.

1. _____ Nado en la piscina los lunes.

2. _____ Miro la televisión los martes.

3. _____ El jueves voy al café con David.

4. _____ Cristóbal va a trabajar el domingo.

5. _____ Voy al parque el sábado.

6. _____ Hoy es miércoles.

22 Sofie is trying to make plans with her friend Alex, who is always busy. Fill in the blanks with **el** or **los** to complete each sentence. In one blank, you won't need an article. Mark an **X** in that blank.

SOFIE   **(1)** _____ viernes, voy a comer con mis papás. Vamos a celebrar mi cumpleaños *(birthday)*. ¿Quieres ir con nosotros?

ALEX   Gracias, pero no puedo. **(2)** _____ viernes siempre estudio música.

SOFIE   Vale. Oye, ¿qué haces **(3)** _____ sábado?

ALEX   **(4)** _____ sábados voy al cine con mi primo Carlos.

SOFIE   ¿Y esta noche?

ALEX   Hoy es **(5)** _____ martes; puedo hacer algo contigo.

SOFIE   ¡Excelente! Vamos al parque.

23 Write one or two things you regularly do on the following days of the week.

1. (los lunes) _____

2. (los martes) _____

3. (los viernes) _____

4. (los sábados) _____

5. (los domingos) _____

El ritmo de la vida

■ PRIMER PASO

To discuss how often you do things, you might use the word *never*. Other negative words like *never* are *nothing* and *no one*.

> *G*ramática   Negation   *Pupil's Edition, p. 196*
>
> To make a negative sentence, either put the negative word before the verb *or* put **no** before the verb and the negative word after the verb.
>
> **nunca** *(never, not ever)*   **Nunca** hablo por teléfono.
>
> **No** hablo por teléfono **nunca.**
>
> **nada** *(nothing)*   **No** tengo **nada** en la mochila.
>
> **nadie** *(nobody)*   **Nadie** mira la televisión.
>
> **No** mira la televisión **nadie.**

1 Pepe, a reporter for the school newspaper, is interviewing Rita Ramírez, a star athlete at his school. Read this portion of their interview, underline all of the expressions that tell how often she does the activities she mentions, and then select the option that best completes each sentence according to their conversation.

> **PEPE**   Rita, ¿con qué frecuencia montas en bicicleta?
>
> **RITA**   ¡Monto en bicicleta todos los días!
>
> **PEPE**   ¿Siempre nadas en la piscina también?
>
> **RITA**   No, no siempre, pero nado en la piscina muchas veces durante la semana. Nado sólo cuando tengo tiempo.
>
> **PEPE**   Y Rita, ¿te gusta hablar por teléfono?
>
> **RITA**   ¡No me gusta hablar por teléfono para nada! Nunca hablo por teléfono.

1. Rita siempre _____ .

2. Rita nunca _____ .

3. Rita _____ sólo cuando tiene tiempo.

   a. monta en bicicleta

   b. nada

   c. habla por teléfono

   d. trabaja

   e. dibuja

2 Some of Mr. Edwards' students are very conscientious, but others are not! Complete his descriptions of the students by writing a negative sentence that contrasts with the affirmative ones. The first one has been done for you.

1. Mónica siempre cuida a su hermano los fines de semana. (Silvia / nunca)

   Pero Silvia nunca cuida a su hermano.

2. Alguien estudia en la biblioteca. (nadie / hacer la tarea)

   _____

3. Pablo y Sofía siempre caminan con el perro en el parque. (sus hermanos / nunca / ir al parque)

   _____

4. Todos miran la televisión. (nadie / mirar el Canal 13)

   _____

5. Luis y Fernando siempre van al parque para jugar al tenis. (Ernesto / nunca)

   _____

3 Write sentences telling how often or when you do the following activities.

MODELO   ¿Tocas la guitarra?   **Nunca toco la guitarra.**

1. ¿Miras la televisión?_____

2. ¿Organizas tu cuarto? _____

3. ¿Montas en bicicleta?_____

4. ¿Trabajas con la computadora?_____

5. ¿Practicas deportes? _____

6. ¿Tocas la guitarra?_____

Nota *G*ramatical   ¿quién? and ¿quiénes?   *Pupil's Edition, p. 198*

Use **¿quién?** to ask about one person: **¿Quién** es la chica bonita y baja?
Use **¿quiénes?** to ask about more than one person: **¿Quiénes** son ellos?

4 Ms. Carter is a new high school Spanish teacher at school. Complete her questions about everyone by filling in the blanks with **quién** or **quiénes**.

1. ¿ _____ es el chico moreno?

2. ¿ _____ son las chicas en la oficina?

3. ¿ _____ es la chica alta y morena?

4. ¿ _____ es la profesora alta y rubia?

5. ¿ _____ son los chicos rubios?

6. ¿ _____ es el profesor bajo y guapo?

■ SEGUNDO PASO

To talk about what you and your friends like to do together, you'll need to use **gustar**. To talk about what you do during a typical week, you'll need to use phrases that express how often something happens.

ASÍ SE DICE
Talking about what you and your friends like to do together

Pupil's Edition, p. 203

5 A busload of excited campers is headed for Camp Webegone for the summer. Many campers are chatting about activities they like to do. Complete their conversations with the words from the word box.

me	le	nos	te	le	les

FELICIA   ¡Hola! Me llamo Felicia y éste es mi amigo Roberto. A nosotros (**1**) _____
gusta bucear. ¿A ustedes (**2**) _____ gusta bucear?

JUANITO   Mucho gusto. Soy Juanito y ésta es mi amiga Raquel. A nosotros (**3**) _____
gusta bucear y esquiar. ¿A ustedes (**4**) _____ gusta esquiar?

FELICIA   Bueno, a mí (**5**) _____ gusta mucho, pero a Roberto no (**6**) _____
gusta para nada.

ROBERTO   Sí, sí. A mí (**7**) _____ gusta pescar. Raquel, ¿a ti (**8**) _____
gusta pescar?

RAQUEL   Claro que sí, hombre. También a Juanito y a mí (**9**) _____ gusta mucho
correr por la playa. ¿A ustedes (**10**) _____ gusta correr también?

FELICIA   Sí. A nosotros (**11**) _____ gusta mucho. Oye, vamos a correr esta noche, ¿eh?

VOCABULARIO   Activities   *Pupil's Edition, p. 204*

6 Claudia is writing a rough draft of a composition for Spanish class about her family, but she's gotten her notes all mixed up. Help her out by choosing the best completion for each of her sentences and writing it in the blank.

1. A mi padre le gusta comer _____ .

2. A mi abuela le gusta escribir _____ .

3. A mí me gusta asistir a _____ .

4. A mi hermana Sofía le gusta beber _____ .

5. A mis hermanos y a mí nos gusta leer _____ .

a. una clase de ejercicios aeróbicos

b. cartas

c. un sándwich

d. jugo

e. las tiras cómicas

CAPÍTULO 5 Segundo paso

¡Ven conmigo! Adelante Level 1A, Chapter 5

Grammar and Vocabulary Workbook **39**

HRW material copyrighted under notice appearing earlier in this work.

Nota _G_ramatical   Clarifying with **les gusta(n)**   *Pupil's Edition, p. 206*

Since the pronoun **les** can mean *to them* or *to you (plural)*, add the phrases **a ustedes, a ellos,** or **a ellas** for clarification.

 A ustedes les gusta la clase de español.
 A ellos les gusta asistir a una clase de ejercicios aeróbicos.
 A ellas les gustan las tiras cómicas.

7 Linda's grandparents are asking about what activities Linda and her friends enjoy. Supply Linda's responses for each of the following.

MODELO   ¿Luisa y Juan? (estudiar/biblioteca)   **A ellos les gusta estudiar en la biblioteca.**

1. ¿Miguel y Pablo? (jugar al tenis/parque)

   _____

2. ¿Paula y Teresa? (comer/restaurante)

   _____

3. ¿Nosotros? (asisitir/clase de ejercicios aeróbicos)

   _____

4. ¿Ángela y Silviana? (hacer ejercicio/gimnasio)

   _____

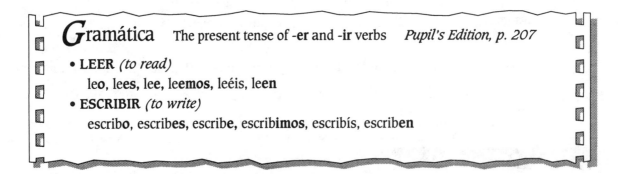

_G_ramática   The present tense of **-er** and **-ir** verbs   *Pupil's Edition, p. 207*

• **LEER** *(to read)*
   le**o**, le**es**, le**e**, le**emos**, le**éis**, le**en**
• **ESCRIBIR** *(to write)*
   escrib**o**, escrib**es**, escrib**e**, escrib**imos**, escrib**ís**, escrib**en**

8 Isabel and Mario are talking about what they and their families do on Saturdays. Complete their conversation by filling in the blanks with the correct form of the verbs in parentheses.

ISABEL Mi hermana Susana siempre **(1)** _____ (escribir) cartas a sus amigos.

 Mis padres y yo **(2)** _____ (comer) en un restaurante cubano. Mis

 hermanos Hernán y Felipe estudian en la biblioteca y yo **(3)** _____ (leer)

 el periódico. ¿**(4)** _____ (leer) tú las tiras cómicas?

MARIO Claro que sí. A ver... durante el día, mi hermana Luisa y yo **(5)** _____

 (asistir) a una clase de ejercicios aeróbicos. Mis padres **(6)** _____ (correr)

 por la playa y mis abuelos **(7)** _____ (hacer) ejercicio en el gimnasio.

9 Patricia has written a short letter to her pen-pal about all of the activities going on this weekend. Complete this portion of her letter by filling in the blanks with the correct form of the verb in parentheses.

¡Hola!

Yo (1) _____ (dibujar) y (2) _____ (montar) en bicicleta. Mi hermano Pablo y yo (3) _____ (caminar) con el perro en el parque. A mi hermana Conchita le gusta (4) _____ (jugar) al tenis con su amiga Gigi. Mi madre (5) _____ (nadar) y (6) _____ (lavar) el carro. Mis hermanos (7) _____ (lavar) la ropa y (8) _____ (hablar) por teléfono. Mis padres (9) _____ (escuchar) música. Mi familia y yo (10) _____ (nadar) y (11) _____ (mirar) la televisión.

Tu amiga,

Patricia

10 Ernesto and Maricarmen have surveyed their classmates to discover some of their typical weekend activities. Complete the students' sentences by deciding which verb fits best in the sentence. Then correctly conjugate the verb.

MODELO   Luis **estudia** (estudiar, bailar) en la biblioteca.

1. Raimundo _____ (escuchar, lavar) la ropa el sábado.

2. Simón y sus padres _____ (hacer, cantar) ejercicio en el gimnasio.

3. Michelle _____ (caminar, cuidar) a sus hermanos.

4. Felipe y yo _____ (montar, regresar) en bicicleta.

5. Teresa _____ (trabajar, bailar) en el supermercado.

6. Silvia y yo _____ (pintar, caminar) con los perros.

7. Bernardo y Lupe _____ (mirar, recibir) la televisión.

8. Soledad _____ (asistir, leer) las tiras cómicas en el periódico.

9. Tú _____ (nadar, escribir) cartas a unos amigos.

10. Yo _____ (beber, bailar) jugo y _____ (comer, cantar) un sándwich.

CAPÍTULO 5 Segundo paso

■ TERCER PASO

To give today's date, you'll need to use numbers and months. To talk about the weather, you'll need to use a variety of weather expressions.

VOCABULARIO Seasons and months *Pupil's Edition, p. 214*

11 One of your responsibilities as secretary of the Spanish Club is to help create the calendar which the club sells every year at their fundraiser. Match the months in the box with the correct season.

> octubre   abril   julio   diciembre   agosto
> junio   mayo   noviembre
> febrero   enero   septiembre   marzo

1. el invierno: _____ _____ _____

2. la primavera: _____ _____ _____

3. el verano: _____ _____ _____

4. el otoño: _____ _____ _____

Nota *G*ramatical Giving today's date *Pupil's Edition, p. 213*

Use the formula **el** + *number* **de** + *month* to give today's date. Use **el primero** for the first day. In Spanish the "on" is omitted in expressions like *on the sixth.*
Hoy es **el veinte de julio.** *Today is July 20th.*
La fiesta es **el diez.** *The party is on the tenth.*

12 Your friend from Spain wants to know when Conchita Martínez will be playing while on tour in the U. S. Write the dates of her tennis matches in Spanish.

1. January 25 _____

2. February 13 _____

3. March 18 _____

4. April 2 _____

5. May 15 _____

6. July 4 _____

7. September 7 _____

8. December 12 _____

¡Ven conmigo! Adelante Level 1A, Chapter 5

13 You've volunteered to help prepare the newsletter for the Hispanic Chamber of Commerce. Your task is to prepare the list of the ten scheduled meetings for this year. In Spanish, write the dates for the following scheduled meetings.

1. January 8 _____

2. February 18 _____

3. March 11 _____

4. April 26 _____

5. May 19 _____

6. June 20 _____

7. July 5 _____

8. August 1 _____

9. September 14 _____

10. October 9 _____

11. November 30 _____

12. December 15 _____

14 Beth works in a very busy office! She's trying to schedule meetings around all the trips everyone will be taking for the next few months. In Spanish, write where each person is going and when he or she plans to leave.

MODELO   María / Cancún / August 4   **María va a Cancún el cuatro de agosto.**

1. Peter / Los Ángeles / February 17

   _____

2. Carol / New York City / March 23

   _____

3. Pablo / Chicago / April 26

   _____

4. Miguel y Bridget / Philadelphia / June 1

   _____

5. Tú / Santiago de Chile / July 18

   _____

6. Bárbara y Abby / Austin, Texas / September 6

   _____

7. Yo / Denver / October 9

   _____

8. Denise / Miami / November 16

   _____

VOCABULARIO   Weather expressions   *Pupil's Edition, p. 216*

15 It's Julio's first day as a weather forecaster and he's arrived late! Help him get ready for his appearance by matching the weather reports in the word box to the weather conditions for the cities listed below.

> Hace frío.   Hace fresco.   Nieva.   Está nublado.
>
> Hace mucho calor.   Hace viento.   Llueve.   Hace sol.

_____ 1. a windy day in Chicago

_____ 2. a bright, sunny day in San Diego

_____ 3. a very hot afternoon in Phoenix

_____ 4. a rainy morning in Seattle

_____ 5. a cloudy day in Milwaukee

_____ 6. a cool evening in Boston

_____ 7. a snowy day in Aspen

_____ 8. a cold morning in Minneapolis

16 Write a description of the weather in the following cities according to the illustrations.

Phoenix

Seattle

Minneapolis

1. En Phoenix _____.

2. En Seattle _____.

3. En Minneapolis _____.

CAPÍTULO 6 Entre familia

■ PRIMER PASO

To describe your family, you'll need to know the names of family members and how to use possessive adjectives.

VOCABULARIO   Family members   *Pupil's Edition, p. 235*

1 Dwayne, an exchange student in La Paz, Bolivia, is describing his family members to his host family. Help with his descriptions by writing the correct family member in each blank below. Some of the choices can be used more than once.

1. La madre de mi madre es mi _____.

2. El hermano de mi madre es mi _____.

3. Mi hermana es la _____ de mis padres.

4. La hija de mi madre y mi padrastro es mi _____.

5. La madre de mi tío es mi _____.

6. La esposa de mi padre que no es mi madre es mi _____.

2 Look at the family tree and tell how these people are related to Ana.

Rebeca Martínez de Cohen – ❤ – Alberto Cohen

León Brodsky – ❤ – Susana Cohen de Brodsky   Esteban Cohen – ❤ – Maureen Hernández de Cohen

Rafael Brodsky   Arturo Brodsky   **Ana Brodsky**   Benjamín Cohen   David Cohen   Lynn Cohen

MODELO   Rebeca Cohen   **Es la abuela de Ana.**

1. Susana Brodsky _____

2. Alberto Cohen _____

3. Esteban Cohen _____

4. Arturo Brodsky _____

5. Maureen Hernández _____

6. León Brodsky _____

7. Rafael Brodsky _____

¡Ven conmigo! Adelante Level 1A, Chapter 6   Grammar and Vocabulary Workbook **45**

CAPÍTULO 6 Primer paso

*G*ramática   Possessive adjectives   *Pupil's Edition, p. 237*

- You already know the singular possessive adjectives:

    mi(s) *(my)*, **tu(s)** *(your)*, and **su(s)** *(his, hers, your)*.

- The plural possessive adjectives are: **nuestro/a(s)** *(our)*, **vuestro/a(s)** *(your-* Spain*)*, and **su(s)** *(your, their)*.
    These adjectives agree in number with the nouns they modify.

    Nuestro**s** amigo**s** miran la televisión.

    Su**s** hermana**s** escuchan la radio.

- Remember that **nuestro** and **vuestro** also agree in gender with the nouns they are modifying.

    Silvia es nuestr**a** herman**a** y nuestr**as** prim**as** son Eva y Julia.

3 Felipe invited some friends to his family reunion. Help him introduce his family members to his friends by circling the possessive adjective that correctly completes each sentence.

1. Ésta es (mi, mis) hermanastra Bianca.

2. Ellos son (mi, mis) abuelos.

3. Éste es (mi, mis) hermano José Antonio.

4. Éstos son (nuestro, nuestra, nuestros, nuestras) primos Pablo y Luisa.

5. Éstas son (nuestro, nuestra, nuestros, nuestras) primas Annick y Yamilé.

6. Ésta es mi tía Lidia, y éstos son (su, sus) hijos.

4 Alexis is on vacation with her family, but everyone misses something from home. Complete each of her sentences with the correct form of the possessive adjective.

1. Mis hermanos quieren _____ tiras cómicas. No quieren leer novelas.

2. Yo quiero _____ traje de baño *(bathing suit)* porque quiero nadar en el lago.

3. Marcos quiere _____ radio porque quiere escuchar música.

4. Nosotros queremos _____ videojuegos que están en casa.

5. Iris y Sandra quieren _____ revistas que dejaron *(they left)* en casa.

6. Quiero ver a _____ mejores amigos Sara y Felipe porque quiero hablar un poco con ellos.

7. Tú quieres _____ zapatillas de tenis para jugar al tenis con Ana.

8. Mi hermana y yo queremos _____ novelas porque no tenemos nada que leer.

■ SEGUNDO PASO

To describe someone, you'll need to use decriptive words and expressions. To discuss activities a family can do together, you'll often need to use the verbs **hacer** and **salir** and the personal **a.**

VOCABULARIO   Descriptive words and expressions   *Pupil's Edition, p. 245*

5 Liza and Lucas are twins. Complete each sentence with an appropriate adjective.

MODELO   Liza es alta. → Lucas también es **alto.**

1. Liza es pelirroja y un poco gorda. Lucas también es _____

   y un poco _____ .

2. Liza es cariñosa. Lucas también es _____ .

3. Lucas es muy listo. Liza también es muy _____ .

4. Liza es traviesa. Lucas también es _____ .

5. Lucas es guapo. Liza también es _____ .

6 Alicia is writing a letter to her pen pal Pilar describing her friends. Fill in the blanks with the correct form of the adjective in parentheses.

Hola Pilar:

Mi amigo Guillermo es (1) _____ (bajo), con ojos

(2) _____ (azul). Su hermana Cora también es

(3) _____ (bajo), pero ella tiene ojos de color

café. Sonja es (4) _____ (guapo) y un poco

(5) _____ (travieso). Megan es

(6) _____ (pelirrojo) y tiene ojos

(7) _____ (verde). Mi amigo Narciso es

(8) _____ (alto) y muy (9) _____

(delgado). Sus hermanas Patricia y Merche también son muy

(10) _____ (alto).

Tu amiga,

Alicia

CAPÍTULO 6 Segundo paso

7 Hiroshi and his sister Umeko never agree on anything! Read Hiroshi's descriptions of the following people, then rewrite the sentences the way Umeko would respond.

MODELO —La hermana de Steve es delgada.

—¡Qué va! *(No way!)* **La hermana de Steve es un poco gorda.**

1. —Francisco es muy joven.

—¡Qué va! _____.

2. —Helen es mayor que Lisa.

—¡Qué va! _____.

3. —Pablo es un poco gordo.

—¡Qué va! _____.

4. —Sofía tiene pelo negro.

—¡Qué va! _____.

5. —Éric tiene ojos de color café.

—¡Qué va! _____.

---

*G*ramática   The verbs **hacer** and **salir**   *Pupil's Edition, p. 249*

- The verb **hacer** *(to make, to do)* is conjugated as follows:

yo	**hago**	nosotros	**hacemos**
tú	**haces**	vosotros	hacéis
él/ ella/ Ud.	**hace**	ellos/ ellas/ Uds.	**hacen**

- The verb **salir** *(to go out)* is conjugated as follows:

yo	**salgo**	nosotros	**salimos**
tú	**sales**	vosotros	salís
él/ ella/ Ud.	**sale**	ellos/ ellas/ Uds.	**salen**

---

8 Latwanda is describing what she and her friends do during the week. Fill in the blanks with the correct forms of **hacer** or **salir.**

1. Los lunes yo _____ mi tarea antes de cenar.

2. Roy _____ con sus amigos los viernes.

3. Torrence, Odessa y yo _____ nuestra tarea juntos en la biblioteca.

4. Anthony, Marvella, y Sarah _____ con sus amigos los sábados. Les gusta ver películas nuevas.

5. Beatriz casi nunca _____ su tarea con nosotros porque siempre estudia sola *(alone)*.

6. Durante el invierno, mi familia y yo siempre _____ un viaje a Aspen.

7. ¿ _____ tú y tu familia algo durante el invierno?

9 Write the questions that would have caused Cindy to give the following responses:

1. ¿_____?

   Los lunes hago mi tarea antes de cenar.

2. ¿_____?

   En general, estudio en la biblioteca los sábados.

3. ¿_____?

   Sí, mi familia y yo hacemos un viaje todos los veranos.

4. ¿_____?

   Sí, Juan y Luisa salen juntos.

Nota *G*ramatical   Personal **a**   *Pupil's Edition, p. 250*

The personal **a** is used when the direct object is a person.
   Visito **a** mi abuela en Francia todos los veranos.
When the direct object is a place or a thing, the **a** is not used.
   Siempre visito la torre Eiffel cuando estoy en París.

---

10 Ernesto has written a letter to his friend Eli. Sometimes it is difficult to tell whether he is talking about a person, place or thing. Fill in the blanks where needed with the personal **a**. Mark an X in the blank if the sentence does not need a personal **a**.

Hola Eli:

Cada verano visito (1) _____ mis abuelos en Miami. El viernes, voy a

visitar (2) _____ la Calle Ocho. Llamo (3) _____ mis

padres casi todos los sábados. Este domingo, voy a visitar (4) _____

los Cayos de la Florida. Vamos a visitar (5) _____ mis tíos que viven

allí. Quiero conocer (6) _____ la nueva esposa de mi tío Mario.

Estoy tan ocupado que no tengo tiempo para mirar (7) _____ la

televisión o escuchar (8) _____ la radio. Y tú, Eli, ¿cómo pasas

(9) _____ tus vacaciones?

Hasta pronto,

Ernesto

■ TERCER PASO

To discuss problems and give advice, you'll need to use the verb **deber.** You also may want to talk about household chores and use the verb **poner.**

> Nota $\mathcal{G}$ramatical The verb **deber** *Pupil's Edition, p. 255*
>
> The verb **deber** *(should, ought to)* is conjugated as follows:
>
> | | |
> |---|---|
> | yo **debo** | nosotros **debemos** |
> | tú **debes** | vosotros debéis |
> | él/ ella/ Ud. **debe** | ellos/ ellas/ Uds. **deben** |

11 Tamika and her friends are telling each other what they think people should do to lead a healthier life. Fill in each blank with the correct form of the verb **deber.**

TAMIKA   Tú (1) _____ practicar un deporte como la natación.

DESIRÉE   Silvia (2) _____ descansar más.

CARMEN   Creo que Ann y Pedro no (3) _____ trabajar tanto.

MIGUEL   Sí, es cierto. Ellos (4) _____ ir de vacaciones.

STANLEY   Todos nosotros (5) _____ pasar más tiempo con la familia y menos en la oficina.

12 Use **deber** and the phrases provided in the box to create five sentences about what these people should do become better students.

> estudiar con los amigos   hablar menos en clase   escuchar más al profesor
>
> hacer toda la tarea   estudiar en la biblioteca   organizar los papeles

1. Yo _____

2. Tú _____

3. Mi amigo _____

4. Nosotros _____

5. Ustedes _____

6. Mis compañeros de clase _____

VOCABULARIO   Household chores   *Pupil's Edition, p. 256*

13 Rearrange the letters in the boxes to reveal what chores everyone has to do.

1. Yo necesito | RTAORC LE ÉDECSP. | _____

2. Manolo debe | NAARHCLP | su ropa. _____

3. Liselotte quiere | MPIIARL AL IACNOC. | _____

4. Juan va a | SAPAR AL DARORAIPAS | en la sala._____

5. Jamyce quiere | BRATARAJ NE LE DNARJÍ. | _____

6. Federico necesita | CHAER AL MCAA. | _____

7. Melissa va a | RACIUD LA TAGO | de su amigo Pablo. _____

8. Diego debe | NOPRE AL SAME | antes de cenar. _____

14 You overhear Carlos and his friends talking about what they do to help out around the house. Fill in each blank with a correct verb to complete their conversation.

JEANNIE   Todos los días, mi prima **(1)** _____ la mesa antes de cenar.

CARLOS   Después de comer, mi hermano Mikel y yo **(2)** _____ la cocina.

FELIX   Mis hermanas y yo no ayudamos en la cocina. Nosotros siempre

(3) _____ la ropa.

ANDRÉS   Yo **(4)** _____ en el jardín con mi papá.

KELLY   Mi hermanastra Cathi **(5)** _____ la aspiradora, pero yo

(6) _____ la cama.

15 Use the clues below to write a sentence about what each person needs to do tonight.

MODELO   Hernán tiene dos gatos, Frijoles y Frankie.
          Hernán debe cuidar a los gatos.

1. A mí me gusta plantar flores *(flowers)*.

   _____

2. Javier necesita arreglar *(to arrange)* su cuarto.

   _____

3. Mamá quiere trabajar afuera. *(outside)*

   _____

4. Don va a limpiar la sala.

   _____

5. Tú quieres vestirte *(dress)* bien mañana.

   _____

¡Ven conmigo! Adelante Level 1A, Chapter 6   Grammar and Vocabulary Workbook **51**

HRW material copyrighted under notice appearing earlier in this work.

Nota *G*ramatical   hacer, salir, and poner   *Pupil's Edition, pp. 249, 257*

The present tense of **hacer, salir,** and **poner** is regular in all but the **yo** form:

	hago	**salgo**	**pongo**
yo	hago	salgo	pongo
tú	haces	sales	pones
él, ella, usted	hace	sale	pone
nosotros	hacemos	salimos	ponemos
vosotros	hacéis	salís	ponéis
ellos, ellas, ustedes	hacen	salen	ponen

16 Change the following sentences to agree with each new subject.

1. Marcos hace la cama antes de salir.

   Tú _____.

2. Nosotros salimos juntos los viernes.

   Wei y Cristina nunca_____.

3. Los muchachos ponen la mesa los lunes y los jueves.

   Yo _____.

4. Édgar hace la tarea antes de mirar la televisión.

   Julieta y yo _____.

5. Ricardo sale con Mark y Rebecca.

   Yo _____.

6. Yo pongo la ropa en el armario.

   Ustedes _____.

17 Conjugate the verbs to create sentences about what these people do on the weekend.

1. Jimmy / poner / la ropa / en el armario

   _____

2. Mis amigas y yo / salir / todos los sábados

   _____

3. Tú / siempre / poner / la mesa / en casa

   _____

4. Lorna / hacer / la tarea / en la biblioteca

   _____

5. Raúl y Toño / hacer / la cama / en su cuarto

   _____

HRW material copyrighted under notice appearing earlier in this work.